BODYGUARDS

By Antony Loveless

CRABTREE
Publishing Company
www.crabtreebooks.com

The World's MOST DANGEROUS Jobs

Editors: Mark Sachner, Adrianna Morganelli
Editorial director: Kathy Middleton
Proofreader: Redbud Editorial
Production coordinator: Margaret Salter
Prepress technician: Margaret Salter
Project director: Ruth Owen
Designer: Elaine Wilkinson
Cover design: Alix Wood

Photo credits:
Corbis: Robert Sciarrino: pages 14-15; Brooks Kraft: page 22 (top)
James Dale: page 25
Department of Defense: front cover (top), pages 5, 21
Getty Images: Chip Somodevilla/Staff: front cover (bottom);
    Jim Watson: page 22 (bottom)
Antony Loveless: page 1, 7, 8, 9, 10–11, 13, 16, 19, 27, 29

COVER STORY

◄ COVER (top) – The former U.S. President and First Lady, George W. Bush and Laura Bush, travel inside of an armoured limousine flanked by Secret Service Agents during the time of his presidency.

◄ COVER (bottom) – Secret Service agents surround U.S. President Barack Obama at a public appearance.

PAGE 1 – Bodyguards in "Little Bird" helicopters protect a United States official in Iraq.

Library and Archives Canada Cataloguing in Publication

Loveless, Antony
    Bodyguards / Antony Loveless.

(The world's most dangerous jobs)
Includes index.
ISBN 978-0-7787-5094-9 (bound).--ISBN 978-0-7787-5108-3 (pbk.)

    1. Bodyguards--Juvenile literature.
I. Title. II. Series: World's most dangerous jobs

HV8290.L69 2009   j363.28'9   C2009-903849-8

Library of Congress Cataloging-in-Publication Data

Loveless, Antony.
    Bodyguards / Antony Loveless.
      p. cm. -- (The world's most dangerous jobs)
    Includes index.

    ISBN 978-0-7787-5108-3 (pbk. : alk. paper) -- ISBN 978-0-7787-5094-9
(reinforced library binding : alk. paper)
    1. Bodyguards--Juvenile literature. 2. Bodyguards--United States--Juvenile
literature. I. Title.
    HV8290.L68 2010
    363.28'9--dc22
                                          2009024551

Published in Canada
Crabtree Publishing
616 Welland Ave.
St. Catharines, ON
L2M 5V6

Published in the United States
Crabtree Publishing
PMB16A
350 Fifth Ave., Suite 3308
New York, NY 10118

Published in the United Kingdom
Crabtree Publishing
Lorna House, Suite 3.03, Lorna Road
Hove, East Sussex, UK
BN3 3EL

Published in Australia
Crabtree Publishing
386 Mt. Alexander Rd.
Ascot Vale (Melbourne)
VIC 3032

CONTENTS

BODYGUARDS

In today's world, most people are unlikely to take part in dangerous activities during their day at work. They sit at desks in offices, or they work in shops and factories.

For bodyguards, living with danger is very much a part of their everyday life. Bodyguards go to work to protect the lives of other people. If necessary, they will risk their own lives to protect their "principal"—the person they have been hired to look after.

A bodyguard will shadow their principal wherever he or she goes. Sometimes that means lots of travel and long periods of time away from home. A bodyguard will sometimes know important or private details about the principal's life. A bodyguard must never disclose this information.

Bodyguards work for police, military, or **civilian** organizations. Many celebrities hire bodyguards, but these big, burly men are usually just for show. United States Secret Service bodyguards or the police bodyguards who look after the UK royal family adopt a much lower profile. They are armed and well trained, but they do their job without show or fuss.

Bodyguards can carry a weapon, such as a gun, but they have no legal right to use force unless they or their principal are attacked.

▲ United States Secret Service agents flank the President's limousine

THE DANGERS

The work that bodyguards do is known as "close protection." If the worst happens, a bodyguard's role is simple—protect the principal at all costs and with your own life if necessary.

In 1981, John Hinckley, Jr., shot President Ronald Reagan. One of the president's Secret Service bodyguards, named Tim McCarthy, used his own body to shield the president. Hinckley fired six bullets at President Reagan. One of the bullets hit McCarthy in the stomach. Another Secret Service agent pushed the president onto the floor of his car and jumped on top of him to protect him. Everyone survived the attack.

When a bodyguard's principal is threatened, the bodyguard has two choices—fight or flight (escape). Wherever possible, flight is the preferred option. Sometimes, though, the bodyguard may need to exchange physical violence or gunfire with the attackers in order to extract their principal from the danger zone.

Bodyguards are often killed while protecting their principals. In many cases, if a principal is killed, one or more of the bodyguards will almost certainly die, too.

▶ Paul Bremer (in dark suit at right), the United States pro consul to Iraq, visits a sports stadium in Baghdad in April 2004. He is flanked by his heavily armed close protection team.

> Most bodyguards admit there is one thing they fear the most. You can have all the training and weaponry in the world, but you can never truly protect your principal against a committed assassin willing to exchange his life for that of his target.
>
> **The bodyguard cannot be identified**

BODYGUARD TRAINING

Bodyguards generally have a background in the armed forces, the police, or security services such as the Central Intelligence Agency (CIA). They are trained in bodyguard skills by the organization they work for. Julian is a bodyguard with the Metropolitan Police in London, in the United Kingdom. He says:

" To work in the world of close protection you must be trained in using firearms. You must also be skilled in the use of other weapons, such as **Tasers** or special sprays, such as **CS Gas**, that can stop an attacker. You will also be trained in unarmed combat. Bodyguards are also trained in **tactical and evasive driving** and advanced first aid. There is an art to providing a protective escort or scanning a crowd for potential threats so we learn how to do this, too.

▲ Bodyguards working in Iraq practice "actions on" during some downtime. "Actions on" is a term used to describe what the bodyguards do in certain situations, such as an **ambush**.

We also learn how to scan for electronic surveillance equipment. For example, we might search a room for a "bug" placed by someone who wants to gain information that will help them to harm the person we are protecting.

What we do can be very physically demanding and the hours can be long. Wherever the principal goes, we go. If the principal runs six miles (ten kilometers) each morning, you have to be able to keep up. Some of the Royals are known for working long hours, so we have to stay focused even if we've been on the go for hours.

You must be able to think fast and change your plans at a moment's notice. For example, if a vehicle is blocking a route you wanted to take, you have to stay calm. You must think clearly and reassure the client while planning ahead. The vehicle might be perfectly innocent, but you can't afford to take anything for granted. On the other hand, you can't go bowling in all guns blazing, either!"

▼ Heavily armed close protection officers from the City of London Police carry out a stop on a suspect vehicle during a training exercise.

BODYGUARD PROFILES AND WEAPONS

There are three different profiles that a Close Protection (CP) team can use. A team's profile is the way it presents itself or makes its presence known in public.

When operating in a hostile environment, such as a war zone, a CP team might adopt a "military overt protection" profile. The bodyguards and their principal will wear body armor over their clothes. The bodyguards will carry weapons in plain sight. An overt profile acts as a deterrent against an attack. The CP team can also react with maximum firepower if required.

▶ A Taser transmits a 50,000-volt electrical pulse through its wires and into the body. This stuns the subject. They are dazed and the lack of muscle control causes them to collapse to the ground where they can be restrained.

Bodyguards sometimes carry non-lethal weapons. These include batons, pepper spray, or Tasers—weapons that give an electric shock.

When a CP team wants to blend into a situation, it uses "low-key overt protection." The U.S. Secret Service uses this profile when the president appears in public. The CP team is visible, but they wear business suits with their weapons concealed beneath their jackets.

A "covert protection" profile means the bodyguards are not visible. They are close by, though, and are ready to react.

If bodyguards are protecting a head of state, they might have automatic machine pistols or even mini submachine guns concealed on their bodies. When bodyguards have to work in dangerous environments, such as Iraq, they may carry assault rifles, such as M-16s and AK-47s.

X26

BODYGUARD EQUIPMENT

A bodyguard who is protecting a high-risk client will often wear body armor. Ceramic plates, which can protect against rifle fire, can be added to the armor.

Bodyguards also use other bullet-proof items to shield their principal. A bodyguard might carry a briefcase that is reinforced with a hard, strong material called Kevlar. The briefcase looks normal but can be opened out and used as a shield.

Sometimes bodyguards carry an extendable steel baton. This can be concealed in the bodyguard's hand. It is used to fight off an attacker at close quarters.

Bodyguards carry medical trauma packs. These include plasma (synthetic blood), **resuscitation kits**, and bandages. This equipment can be used to give immediate first aid if the principal is injured.

Sometimes bodyguards use secure communication system networks, called "secure comms." A bodyguard using secure comms wears an encrypted radio. This is a radio with a scrambled signal. Only those on the network can hear what's being said. Anyone listening in will just hear a lot of noise. The radio has a wire running up to an earpiece. Another wire runs down the bodyguard's sleeve to a secret microphone that is hidden in the bodyguard's left palm.

Bodyguards often wear wrap-around sunglasses. They prevent the crowd from seeing where the bodyguard is looking. They also make the bodyguard appear more intimidating.

Secure comms radio

Equipment vest to hold grenades, additional ammunition, radio, and weapons, such as a Taser or baton

Armored SUV with bullet-proof glass

Loose clothing for easy movement

CARS AND DRIVING TACTICS

Bodyguards use cars that have been adapted to give a high level of protection. They also carry weapons and medical gear in their cars.

"The type of car we use is important—we can't just use any car. It will generally be a large vehicle, with lots of room inside and a powerful engine. Mercedes Benz, Lincoln Continentals, and SUVs such as Chevrolet Suburbans are all good choices. The car will have armored bodywork and bullet-proof glass. The car's gas tank also contains foam. The foam prevents the tank from exploding if the car gets shot at and the tank is hit.

◄ An evasive driving instructor acts as an attacker in a chase car during a bodyguard training class. The student maneuvers through an obstacle course while trying to avoid being hit by a paintball gun.

A vehicle might also be adapted so it is basically a sealed unit. It will then have its own oxygen supply. This would be required to protect against a poisonous gas attack.

If we think an attack is going to happen, we have to get the principal out of the situation and moved to somewhere safe. If we can't go forward, we'll reverse and choose another route. If that option is closed to us, we use what's called offensive driving skills. This is when we use the car as a weapon and ram whatever it is that's blocking our way. Sometimes the cars we use have reinforced bumpers to make the car doubly effective at doing this. Sometimes we use another car in the convoy to block the attacker's vehicle. This helps us get the principal's car away from danger."

John, Bodyguard, U.S. Marshals Service

▲ Three Special Escort Group motorcyclists ride in an arrowhead formation.

SPECIAL ESCORT GROUP

In the United Kingdom, the security of the **sovereign** and other members of the royal family is entrusted to The Royalty and Diplomatic Protection Department of the Metropolitan Police. This police department also protects important foreign visitors when they visit the U.K.

Specially trained police bodyguards, known as the Royalty Protection Group (SO14), protect the Queen and other members of the royal family.

The Royalty and Diplomatic Protection Department is responsible for handling all escorts and motorcades. Officers from the department's Special Escort Group (SEG) carry out this work. The SEG officers are highly trained, armed motorcycle guards who escort principals as outriders in front of or alongside a motorcade.

Some of the biggest potential threats to the safety of principals occur when their car is stationary. A motorcade stuck in gridlocked traffic is a security risk. Therefore, it's the SEG's job to keep the motorcade moving.

When SEG officers escort the Queen, the Prime Minister, and other important people, such as government ministers and visiting heads of state, through heavy London traffic, they don't stop—for anyone!

SPECIAL ESCORT GROUP IN ACTION

Police Constable Peter Skerrit has been with the UK's Special Escort Group for 20 years. He has escorted some of the most famous and important people in the world, from Princess Diana to President George W. Bush.

"Regardless of the length of a motorcade, we only ever use a maximum of four bikes on escort. One rider will sit at the head of a motorcade. This rider sets the pace based on radio messages sent back by three 'working bikes.' The job of the working bikes is to sprint ahead and take control of junctions. As they progress, the bikes leapfrog each other.

The SEG's aim is to move swiftly and in a way that does not inconvenience other road users. Using smooth teamwork, the SEG guides the motorcade through red lights and against the flow of traffic. The motorcade is gone before the drivers of waiting cars have even noticed the delay or who was in the cars. This is also a secure way to travel as nobody really knows about the motorcade until it has gone by.

SEG riders face considerable risks. They need to enter busy junctions, often driving into oncoming traffic that has a green light. The bikes do not have sirens to accompany their flashing blue lights—the officers use whistles instead! It is so noisy in London that most people no longer take notice of sirens. Whistles are a completely alien sound though, so they're very effective."

▼ A member of the Special Escort Group takes control of a junction in front of Buckingham Palace in London. The motorcade at the left of the picture will speed through the junction without stopping.

THE SECRET SERVICE

The United States Secret Service safeguards the lives of the president, the first lady, the president's children, the vice president, and other executive officials. All former presidents also receive Secret Service protection for up to ten years.

"Protecting the President is a very complex task. It extends to more than just having him surrounded by armed agents. Extensive investigation work is carried out in advance of any meetings or events the president attends. Our Intelligence Division does this work. Secret Service agents visit the area to which the president is traveling. They check out hospitals and escape routes in case of an emergency. They decide how many agents will be needed on the day. They also alert all public service departments, such as police forces and fire departments, in the area. Doing this "advance work" cuts down the risk of potential threats.

One of the agents will be appointed to organize and coordinate all the police and other law enforcement officers who will be on site on the day. Checkpoints will be set up in the area to restrict access. A plan of action is drawn up so that if there is an emergency everyone knows what to do, where to go, and how to act. We leave nothing to chance. Everything is planned and rehearsed. There are no surprises."

United States Secret Service Agent

▲ U.S. Secret Service agents flank President Obama and Mrs. Obama as they walk along Pennsylvania Avenue, Washington D.C., following the inauguration in January 2009.

▲ President Obama's Cadillac, "The Beast."

▼ Flanked by Secret Service agents, President Obama goes to talk to the crowd before boarding Air Force One.

PROTECTING PRESIDENT OBAMA

President Barack Obama is protected by at least 200 Secret Service agents. They shadow his every move and are ready to respond with extreme violence should his life be threatened.

" When traveling by road, President Obama is driven in a specially adapted Cadillac. The car is known as 'The Beast.' The car has an armor-plated body. Its bullet-proof glass is so thick that special lighting is needed inside to allow the President to read.

The car's interior is sealed so it's like a 'panic room.' The car is capable of shielding the President from a chemical weapons or biological weapons attack.

The car is equipped with a night-vision camera, pump-action shotguns, tear gas cannons, oxygen tanks, and bottles of the President's blood. Its tires allow it to keep driving even if they have been punctured. "

United States Secret Service Agent

President Obama flies in specially modified Boeing 747 aircraft. There are two such planes, each known as Air Force One. Each luxurious plane has bedrooms, showers, a gym, and work areas. Air Force One is heavily armored with bullet-proof windows. It can withstand a nuclear blast from below.

BODYGUARD ROLES

The United States Marshals Service provides bodyguards who are responsible for the safety of government witnesses and their families. Often, if a person gives evidence in court against a major criminal, such as a drug trafficker or **terrorist**, his or her life might be in danger. Major criminals will stop at nothing to stay free, even if it means killing those brave enough to give **testimony** against them.

The U.S. Marshals Service protects witnesses before and during the trial. After the trial, witnesses will be protected as part of the Witness Protection Program. They'll be moved to a new area and given a new identity with a passport and credit cards in their new name. All of this also occurs under the direction of the U.S. Marshals Service. Nobody in the Witness Protection Program has ever been harmed while under the protection of the U.S. Marshals Service.

Many civilians, such as doctors, news reporters, and charity workers, from the United States, United Kingdom, and other nations are working in war zones such as Iraq and Afghanistan. These people need to be protected. Military forces do not have enough soldiers to offer this protection. Therefore, private military companies offer bodyguard services in these places. The private bodyguard companies work for governments or charities.

▲ Heavily armed private close protection officers prepare for the day alongside an armored SUV in Iraq.

A DAY IN THE LIFE OF A BODYGUARD

Bodyguards often work long shifts to provide 24-hour protection, seven days a week. Close protection for one principal can involve six bodyguards on the day shift and six at night.

"A typical day for us begins a lot earlier than our principal's. We'll have the principal's diary and daily schedule well ahead of time and will have done a lot of legwork (preparation work).

Routes to and from any venues are checked in advance. We also check out any staff at the venue that will have contact with our principal.

The cars are checked well ahead of time. Once inspected, they are brought to whatever door the principal will leave by. One member of the team stays with the cars because once searched, they can't be left unattended.

When it's time to leave, we'll flank our principal as he or she moves from the security of the home to the car. We're always on high alert at this stage because the principal has neither the protection of the secure building, nor the car.

Assuming a clear run, on arrival, several members of the CP team will exit the cars first.

Once the immediate area around the car is clear, we'll escort the principal into the building using a flanking procedure. After the day's activities, it's pretty much the same thing in reverse.

We never stop learning, so there will be a debrief—a meeting where the day's events are talked through. Were any mistakes made? Were there any incidents such as a protester managing to confront the principal?

It's tiring work, no matter how fit you are. Being so focused throughout each day drains you. I always fall straight asleep when I eventually get to bed. "

Ryan, Bodyguard, Royal Military Police

▲ Sir Jeremy Greenstock (third from left, back row), a British official and Special Representative of the Queen, with his Royal Military Police close protection team. This team provided round the clock protection during his time in Iraq.

27

A DAY IN THE LIFE OF A PRINCIPAL

James is an English journalist. In 2004, he was posted to Baghdad, Iraq, to report on the war. James was given a four-man close protection team.

"Whenever I wanted to pursue a story, the CP team would go out in advance and check the route. When we headed out, it would always be in a two-car convoy of armored SUVs. We all wore body armor and the bodyguards carried grenades, submachine guns, and assault rifles.

Traffic in Baghdad was a nightmare, and you're a sitting duck if you're not moving. Route Irish was always the worst. It was the only route to and from the airport, so the insurgents always had it targeted. On one journey along Route Irish we were dodging burnt-out wrecks. As we slowed to pass one, we started taking small arms fire from some bushes at the roadside. Bullets struck the window—which gave me a scare—but they didn't penetrate. As soon as we started taking fire, the driver floored the accelerator. We rammed anything in our path to escape while the guys in the back-up vehicle returned fire. We got away and I eventually got the story I was after, but I won't forget that day in a hurry!

"Whenever we'd get to our destination, the guys would surround me. As we walked, they shielded me. To be honest, I never got used to the idea that I was somehow more important than any of them. I was enormously grateful that they were there, though."

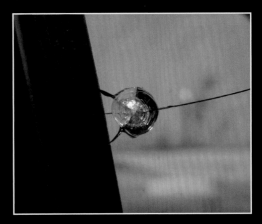

▲ James's car after the attack in Iraq. The bullet-proof glass was effective against the small arms fire.

◄ A private close protection officer stands alongside his armored SUV waiting for James, his principal.

IT'S A FACT!

The weapons a bodyguard can use depends on a nation's laws and which agency the bodyguard is working for. In the United Kingdom, for example, ordinary citizens are not allowed to carry guns. Only military or police bodyguards can use firearms in the UK.

Bullet-proof glass is very thick and heavy. It is usually between four and five inches (10 to 13 centimeters) thick!

United States Secret Service agents wear specially tailored suits that are designed to hide the tell-tale bulge caused by the sidearms that they carry in their shoulder holsters.

President Barack Obama's Secret Service code name is Renegade. The First Lady's code name is Renaissance. The Obama's daughters are known as Rosebud and Radiance. The names are chosen to be easily pronounced and understood when agents are whispering into microphones hidden up their sleeves.

A close protection team might carry gas masks. The gas masks will be worn by the bodyguards and the principal to protect against an attack by dangerous gases or sprays.

Bodyguards online
www.secretservice.gov/
www.usmarshals.gov/
www.met.police.uk/so/protection.htm

GLOSSARY

ambush A surprise attack.

assassin A person who targets and kills a public figure such as a politician or sovereign.

biological weapons Weapons that use bacteria, viruses, or other disease-causing agents to cause widespread death or illness.

chemical weapons Weapons that use toxic chemicals and gases as weapons to kill, injure, or disable an enemy.

civilian A person who is not in a branch of the military, such as the army, air force, or navy, or a member of a law enforcement agency.

CS gas A non-lethal tear gas made from a chemical compound. It takes its name from the initials of the two scientists that discovered it—Ben Corson and Roger Stoughton.

pepper spray A personal defense spray that contains capsaicin, a chemical that comes from chili peppers. Capsaicin irritates the eyes, causing tears, pain, and even temporary blindness.

resuscitation kit A small, lightweight kit containing the medical equipment needed to attempt to revive someone who is not breathing.

sovereign The person who possesses supreme power. In a monarchy, such as the United Kingdom, this will be the King or Queen.

tactical and evasive driving Highly specialized driving skills used by bodyguards. These include braking techniques, skid control maneuvers, and dealing with multiple vehicles that are trying to force another vehicle off the road. The skills also include escape maneuvers, emergency braking and turns, and forward and reverse ramming.

taser A weapon that fires two darts into the body that transmit a high-voltage electrical current to disrupt the victim's control of his or her muscles.

tear gas The term used for any non-lethal gas used defensively. It causes the eyes to run and irritates the nose, eyes, mouth, and lungs. CS gas and pepper spray are both tear gasses.

terrorist A person who tries to frighten people or governments into doing what he or she wants by using violence or the threat of violence.

testimony Facts or a statement that are given as evidence by a witness in a court of law.

INDEX

A

Afghanistan 24
Air Force One 22, 23
armor 10, 12

B

batons 11, 12, 13
Beast, The 22, 23
bodyguards 4, 10, 11, 12,
　24, 25, 26, 27
　military 8, 27, 30
　police 8, 24, 30
　private 8, 24, 25, 28,
　　29
　procedures 26, 27
　profiles 10, 11
Bremer, Paul 7
Buckingham Palace 19
bullet-proof glass 12, 13,
　14, 23, 29, 30

C

Central Intelligence
　Agency (CIA) 8
close protection 6, 8, 10,
　11, 28
CS gas 8, 31

D

dangers 4, 6, 7

E

equipment 12, 13, 30

F

firearms 8, 11, 28
first aid 8, 12

G

Greenstock, Sir Jeremy
　27

H

Hinckley, Jr., John 6

I

Iraq 7, 8, 24, 27, 28, 29

L

London 18, 19

M

McCarthy, Tim 6
Metropolitan Police 8, 9,
　17

O

Obama, First Lady
　Michelle 21, 30
Obama, President Barack
　21, 22, 23, 30

P

pepper spray 11, 31
President of the United
　States 20, 21, 22, 23
principals 4, 6, 7, 9, 12,
　15, 17, 26, 27, 28, 29

R

Reagan, President Ronald
　6
royal family (British) 4, 9,
　17
Royal Military Police 27
Royalty and Diplomatic

Protection Department
　17
Royalty Protection Group
　(SO14) 17

S

Secret Service agents
　(United States) 4, 5, 6,
　11, 20, 21, 22, 23, 30
secure comms 12, 13
Special Escort Group
　(SEG) 16, 17, 18, 19
surveillance work 9

T

tactical and evasive
　driving 8, 9, 14, 15,
　28, 31
Tasers 8, 10, 11, 13, 31
tear gas 23, 31
training 8, 9, 14, 15

U

United States Marshals
　Service 24

V

vehicles 13, 14, 15, 22,
　23, 25, 28, 29

W

Washington D.C. 21
weapons 4, 8, 10, 11, 12,
　13, 14, 23, 28, 30, 31
Witness Protection
　Program 24

Printed in the USA—BG